THE AMAZING MATH JOURNEY

3

A TREASURY OF KNOWLEDGE

www.royalcollins.com

THE AMAZING MATH JOURNEY

3

A TREASURY OF KNOWLEDGE

Written and illustrated by

Youdao Joyread Editorial Board

RC

Books Beyond Boundaries

ROYAL COLLINS

The Amazing Math Journey
Volume 3: A Treasury of Knowledge

Written and illustrated by Youdao Joyread Editorial Board
Editorial Board Members: Yan Jiarui, Cui Yao, and Wang Dandan
Illustrator: Yan Jiarui

First published in 2024 by Royal Collins Publishing Group Inc.
Groupe Publication Royal Collins Inc.
BKM Royalcollins Publishers Private Limited

Headquarters: 550-555 boul. René-Lévesque O Montréal (Québec) H2Z1B1 Canada
India office: 805 Hemkunt House, 8th Floor, Rajendra Place, New Delhi 110 008

ISBN: 978-1-4878-1172-3

To find out more about our publications, please visit www.royalcollins.com.

Preface

What do you think of when you hear the word "math"? A bunch of strange and difficult formulas? Or mysterious and incomprehensible geometric shapes? Or maybe tricky word problems?

This book presents interesting knowledge related to the first two volumes of math stories, covering Chinese and foreign history and culture, astronomy, geography, etc. By reading this book, you will have a new understanding of math.

This book will take you on a journey through the history of math and expand on related scientific and humanistic knowledge, telling you why math is so important to our lives now.

Now, let's start our reading journey!

Instructions for Using This Book

1 Read the stories from the first two volumes of the *Amazing Math Journey*.

Volume 1

Volume 2

2 Chapters 2–8 of the first two volumes correspond to two popular science articles in this book for each chapter.

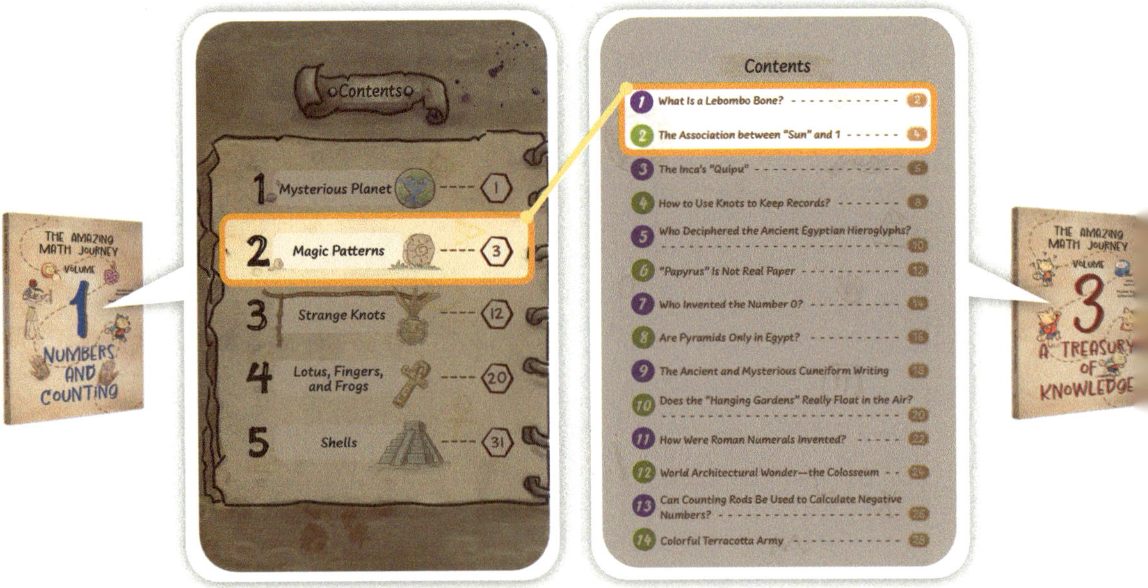

3 After reading a chapter in the story, complete this book's corresponding popular science articles.

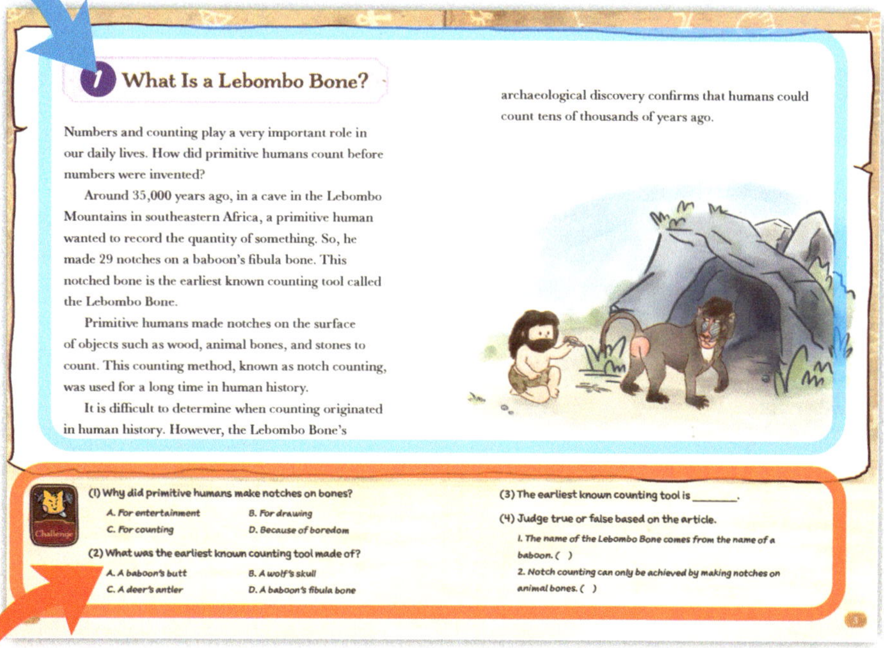

1 What Is a Lebombo Bone?

Numbers and counting play a very important role in our daily lives. How did primitive humans count before numbers were invented?

Around 35,000 years ago, in a cave in the Lebombo Mountains in southeastern Africa, a primitive human wanted to record the quantity of something. So, he made 29 notches on a baboon's fibula bone. This notched bone is the earliest known counting tool called the Lebombo Bone.

Primitive humans made notches on the surface of objects such as wood, animal bones, and stones to count. This counting method, known as notch counting, was used for a long time in human history.

It is difficult to determine when counting originated in human history. However, the Lebombo Bone's archaeological discovery confirms that humans could count tens of thousands of years ago.

Challenge

(1) Why did primitive humans make notches on bones?

A. For entertainment B. For drawing
C. For counting D. Because of boredom

(2) What was the earliest known counting tool made of?

A. A baboon's butt B. A wolf's skull
C. A deer's antler D. A baboon's fibula bone

(3) The earliest known counting tool is ________.

(4) Judge true or false based on the article.

1. The name of the Lebombo Bone comes from the name of a baboon. ( )
2. Notch counting can only be achieved by making notches on animal bones. ( )

4 Test yourself after reading and try to answer the challenge questions at the bottom of each popular science article.

5 Check the electronic version of the answers carefully and think deeply to better understand.

Please refer to our website if you'd like to check the answers to the "challenges." (www.royalcollins.com/answer-key-of-a-treasury-of-knowledge)

Contents

A TREASURY OF KNOWLEDGE
Challenge
Mathematics
Astronomy
History
Geography

1 What Is a Lebombo Bone?

Numbers and counting play a very important role in our daily lives. How did primitive humans count before numbers were invented?

Around 35,000 years ago, in a cave in the Lebombo Mountains in southeastern Africa, a primitive human wanted to record the quantity of something. So, he made 29 notches on a baboon's fibula bone. This notched bone is the earliest known counting tool called the Lebombo Bone.

Primitive humans made notches on the surface of objects such as wood, animal bones, and stones to count. This counting method, known as notch counting, was used for a long time in human history.

It is difficult to determine when counting originated in human history. However, the Lebombo Bone's

Challenge

(1) Why did primitive humans make notches on bones?

A. For entertainment
B. For drawing
C. For counting
D. Because of boredom

(2) What was the earliest known counting tool made of?

A. A baboon's butt
B. A wolf's skull
C. A deer's antler
D. A baboon's fibula bone

archaeological discovery confirms that humans could count tens of thousands of years ago.

(3) The earliest known counting tool is ________.

(4) Judge true or false based on the article.

1. The name of the Lebombo Bone comes from the name of a baboon. (   )

2. Notch counting can only be achieved by making notches on animal bones. (   )

2 The Association between "Sun" and 1

People discovered only one sun in the sky in ancient times, so they used "sun" to represent 1. When people want to express that there is only one thing, they say it is as many as the "sun."

The association between "sun" and 1 is thus preserved. In modern language and culture, we can still find a close relationship between the two.

Latin is the mother of European languages, and 70% to 80% of English words have roots in Latin. In Latin, "sun" is represented as "sol." In English, the word root "sol-" not only means "related to the sun," but also means "alone" and "unique." For example, the English word "soloist" means "a solo performer," while "solo" means "alone."

Challenge

(1) Why did primitive people use "sun" to represent 1? Judge true or false based on the article.

1. Because the sun is big and dazzling. ( )

2. Because there is only one sun. ( )

It can be seen that in the vocabulary of modern language, we can also find traces of ancient counting thinking, thus understanding the deeper meanings of vocabulary.

(2) Judge true or false based on the article.

1. The root of all English words comes from Latin. ( )

2. Latin is the mother of all languages. ( )

(3) Guess the meaning of the English word "solitary."

A. Together *B. United*

C. Alone *D. All*

3 The Inca's "Quipu"

The Ancient Inca people in Peru used the hair of alpacas and lamini (a subspecies similar to llamas and alpacas) to make strings, which were then knotted in a specific way to count or record events. This method is called "quipu," which means "knot" in the Quechua language.

Quipus could record various numerical matters in the Inca people's lives, such as the amount of stored agricultural products, population size, and important dates.

When counting with quipus, the different shapes, colors, and arrangements of the knots on the strings represented different meanings. However, the exact meanings behind the various knots have yet to be deciphered.

(1) What material did the Ancient Inca people use to make strings?

A. Lamini

B. Straw

C. Hair of alpacas

D. Hair

Scientists have created corresponding databases for each group of quipus, detailing various aspects such as the size, length, and color of the strings, the number of tassels, the number of knots, the age, rotation direction, and rotation frequency of each strand. They hope to discover the rules behind quipus through data analysis and decipher their accurate information.

(2) The method of knotting strings invented by the Ancient Inca people in Peru to count or record events is called _____.

(3) Judge true or false based on the article.

1. Quipus are just random knots on the string. ( )

2. The colors of the string are not required for quipus. ( )

4 How to Use Knots to Keep Records?

Although knot-tying as a method of record-keeping has disappeared into the river of history as an ancient method until the 20th century, we can still find the use of knot-tying for record-keeping in the daily lives of some ethnic minorities in China.

Before the 1950s, the Hani people (found in Yunnan Province in China and neighboring area in Vietnam) used knot-tying to record field prices. When buying or selling land, they often tied a single strand of hemp rope into knots, each representing 1 tael of silver. The buyer and seller had to make two identical ropes, each holding one as a trading voucher.

The Derung people (in Yunnan Province, southwest China) often used knot-tying to record dates. When inviting friends and family, they used two thin ropes and tied an equal number of knots. Each side kept one,

Challenge

(1) When the Hani people bought or sold land and tied a hemp rope into six segments, what was the price of the land in taels of silver?

A. 6 taels of silver　　B. 5 taels of silver

C. 7 taels of silver　　D. 8 taels of silver

(2) What did the Derung people commonly use knot-tying to record?

and they untied one knot every day. When both sides had untied all the knots, they would meet at the agreed-upon place on time.

In today's highly advanced scientific and technological age, we generally do not have to worry about forgetting past events and future tasks because there are tools everywhere that we can use to keep track of things. However, if you can travel back to the time of knot-tying for record-keeping, and all you have is a rope, how would you keep track of your daily life?

A. Number of people

B. Price

C. Date

D. Friends

(3) Judge true or false based on the article.

1. *Knot-tying for record-keeping only existed in ancient times. (   )*
2. *Knot-tying for record-keeping only existed in the daily lives of ethnic minorities. (   )*

5 Who Deciphered the Ancient Egyptian Hieroglyphs?

The British Museum in London has a treasure known as the Rosetta Stone. The French linguistic genius Jean-François Champollion successfully deciphered the Ancient Egyptian hieroglyphs based on the inscriptions on this stone.

The Rosetta Stone is engraved with the same content in three different scripts. The first script is the Ancient Egyptian hieroglyphs, also known as the "sacred book style"; the second script is a simplified version of the Ancient Egyptian script, known as the "common style"; and the third script is Greek. Based on the corresponding relationship between the content of these three scripts on the stone, Champollion started with the symbols representing names and discovered that when the Ancient Egyptians wrote the name of the pharaoh (the title of the king of Ancient Egypt), they spelled it

(1) Based on the article's content, which inferences about Ancient Egyptian writing are correct?

A. Ancient Egyptian writing is like drawing, with each symbol representing a meaning.

B. Ancient Egyptian writing is like spelling in Hanyu Pinyin, with each symbol corresponding to a letter.

C. The names of people in Ancient Egyptian writing are spelled out in a way similar to Hanyu Pinyin.

out using hieroglyphs in a similar way to spell Chinese in Hanyu Pinyin. He found that the Ancient Egyptian hieroglyphs were a type of writing that conveyed both meaning and sound.

After over 20 years of effort, Champollion deciphered the Ancient Egyptian hieroglyphs in 1822. The publication of this research marked the birth of Egyptology, and Champollion was henceforth known as the "Father of Egyptology."

Jean-François Champollion

The Rosetta Stone

D. The changes in Egyptian writing from ancient times to today are insignificant.

(2) ______ is known as the "Father of Egyptology."

(3) Judge true or false based on the article.

1. Ancient Egyptian hieroglyphs are a form of Hanyu Pinyin. ( )
2. The Rosetta Stone is currently located in a museum in Egypt. ( )

6 "Papyrus" Is Not Real Paper

Around 3000 BC, the Ancient Egyptians began manufacturing and using a writing material called "papyrus."

The process of making papyrus is as follows: the Ancient Egyptians first harvested the pith of the papyrus plant on the banks of the river, cut the papyrus into thin slices, and soaked them. Then, they arranged the thin slices horizontally and vertically, stacked them in two layers, and made the directions of the plant fibers perpendicular to each other. Finally, they sandwiched the two layers of thin slices between two wooden boards, pounded, squeezed, dehydrated, dried, and polished them to make papyrus.

The production of Ancient Egyptian papyrus has similarities with papermaking, both of which use the rich fibers in the raw materials to integrate them into sheet-like objects. However, the ways of integration are different: when making papyrus, the fibers of two layers of thin slices need

Challenge

(1) According to the article's content, which of the following descriptions of papyrus is incorrect?

A. Papyrus originated from Ancient Egypt.

B. The main raw material for making papyrus is the pith from the papyrus plant.

C. Papyrus is not real paper.

D. When making papyrus, the thin slices should be arranged in the same direction.

to be directly squeezed together, similar to weaving. On the other hand, papermaking breaks the hydrogen bond links between cellulose molecules through pulping, papermaking, and dehydration, forms new hydrogen bond links, and constructs a strong network structure.

Therefore, the flexibility of papyrus is not enough, and it is not easy to preserve and is often damaged. Most professional scholars believe papyrus is not real paper and can only be called "primitive weaving."

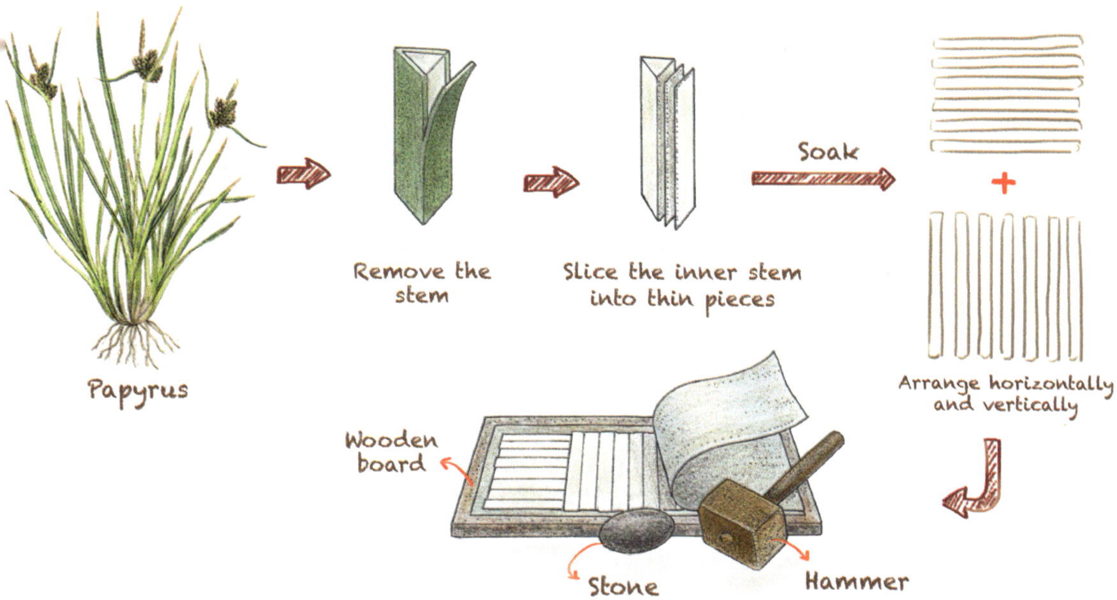

(2) The biggest difference between the production of papyrus and papermaking is ( ).

A. The use of different raw materials

B. Different styles and shapes of the finished product

C. Different ways of integrating raw materials

(3) Judge true or false based on the article.

1. Making papyrus is the same as papermaking in China. ( )

2. When making papyrus, cellulose molecules are not broken apart. ( )

7 Who Invented the Number 0?

The invention of 0 is considered one of the greatest achievements of mankind, making it an extremely important number.

In the 3rd century BC, the Mesopotamians first created the symbol "0." Unfortunately, at that time, "0" was just a character and was not assigned any mathematical meaning.

In the 4th century AD, the Ancient Maya were the first to represent "0" in their counting system. The "0" they represented was a pictograph in the shape of a shell, but at this point, "0" had not yet entered into calculations.

Ancient Indians invented the standardized numeral "0" with mathematical meaning around the 5th century AD. They initially used a black dot to represent zero, and later the dot gradually evolved into "0." In the 7th

(1) What did the "0" invented by the Ancient Maya look like?

A. A space

B. A black dot

C. A pictograph in the shape of a shell

D. The modern number 0

century AD, the Indian mathematician Brahmagupta first fully described 0 as a number, and the number 0 began to be used in practical mathematical calculations.

So, who was the first to invent the number 0? This question has no simple answer because different civilizations have expanded on this concept over thousands of years. It can be said that the invention of the number 0 is a collective wisdom of humanity.

(2) The standardized numeral "0" with mathematical meaning was first invented by ________.

(3) Judge true or false based on the article.

1. *The Arabs invented the number 0. ( )*

2. *The Ancient Indians used "0" to represent the number 0 from the beginning. ( )*

8 Are Pyramids Only in Egypt?

Regarding pyramids, everyone knows that they are the iconic buildings of Egypt. However, pyramids are not unique to Egypt. There are pyramids in other parts of the world, built by civilizations from different regions at different times.

Among various pyramids, the Mayan pyramids are second only to the Egyptian pyramids in popularity. The Mayan pyramids are relatively short, made of stacked boulders, and are grayish white. This kind of pyramid is partially cone-shaped because there is a temple for worshipping gods at its top.

Chichen Itza was once the most prosperous city-state of the Mayan civilization, located on the Yucatan Peninsula in southeastern Mexico. The city's central building is a huge pyramid called the Kukulkan Pyramid, which stands on clear ground in the tropical

Challenge

(1) What are the characteristics of the Mayan pyramids? Choose the option that does not apply.

A. Made of stacked stones

B. Golden yellow in appearance

C. Not completely cone-shaped

D. Generally have a temple at the top

jungle. This pyramid was built between the 11th and 13th centuries and covered an area of about 3,000 square meters. It is the tallest building in Chichen Itza.

Not only are there pyramids on land, but humans have also discovered pyramids on the seabed. The most famous underwater pyramid is located in the Bermuda Triangle. It is said to be related to the lost empire of Atlantis. In terms of volume alone, it is larger than Egypt's Great Pyramid of Giza.

Therefore, pyramids are not unique buildings in Egypt. Their shapes can be found in many cultural relics and historical sites worldwide.

(2) The name of the tallest building in Chichen Itza is ______.

(3) Judge true or false based on the article.

1. The Kukulkan Pyramid is the tallest pyramid in the world. (   )

2. So far, all discovered pyramids have been on land. (   )

9 The Ancient and Mysterious Cuneiform Writing

So far, the three oldest known writings in the world are Sumerian cuneiform, Ancient Egyptian hieroglyphs, and Chinese oracle bone script. Among these three writings, the oldest one is Sumerian cuneiform.

In 3200 BC, the Sumerians who lived in the southern part of the Tigris and Euphrates Rivers created cuneiform writing. They used reeds or bone and wooden sticks sharpened into triangular tips as writing tools to write on damp clay tablets. The shape of the characters naturally formed into wedges (in Latin, cuneus); therefore, this type of writing is called "cuneiform."

To preserve the clay tablets for a long time, the Sumerians dried them before firing. These fired clay tablets were resistant to insect damage, rot, and even fire. However, the tablets were also heavy, weighing

Challenge

(1) According to the article's content, which description of cuneiform is incorrect? ( )

A. Cuneiform is the oldest known writing system so far.

B. Cuneiform is mainly written on clay tablets.

C. Cuneiform is still in use today.

D. Cuneiform was invented earlier than Chinese characters.

about 1 kilogram each, and people had to put in effort to move them around. Up to now, 500,000 to 2,000,000 cuneiform clay tablets have been excavated, with the largest one measuring 2.7 meters long and 1.95 meters wide, truly a "giant book."

Although cuneiform is the oldest writing system in the world, like Ancient Egyptian hieroglyphs, it has been sealed in history and is no longer used. Chinese characters are the only classical writing system passed down and used to this day.

Clay tablet

(2) The oldest writing system in the world is ( ).

A. Cuneiform

B. Ideographic

C. Hieroglyphic

D. Oracle bone script

(3) Judge true or false based on the article.

1. Cuneiform is often recorded on clay tablets. ( )

2. Chinese characters are the only classical writing system passed down and used to this day. ( )

10 Does the "Hanging Gardens" Really Float in the Air?

The Babylonian civilization is one of the four ancient civilizations in the world, and its architecture is unique. The "Hanging Gardens" and "Tower of Babel" in Babylon are wonders of world architectural history. Among them, Babylon's "Hanging Gardens" are listed as one of the eight wonders of the world.

Does the "Hanging Gardens" really float in mid-air? Of course not. It is said that the "Hanging Gardens" used three-dimensional gardening techniques and placed the garden on four terraces, using stone pillars and slabs to stack up to the sky. From afar, the garden appears floating in mid-air, hence the name "Hanging Gardens."

However, unfortunately, like other famous buildings of the Babylonian civilization, the "Hanging Gardens" has long been submerged in the rolling yellow sand

Challenge

(1) Which of the following statements about Babylon's "Hanging Gardens" is correct? ( )

A. Part of it is still available for the visit.

B. It floats in mid-air.

C. It, along with the Tower of Babel, is listed among the eight wonders of the world.

D. People imagine its current appearance.

and no longer exists. The "Hanging Gardens" we know today is speculated from historical records in later generations.

(2) The Babylonian architecture _____ was listed as one of the eight wonders of the world.

(3) Judge true or false based on the article.

1. The Tower of Babel in Babylonian architecture is one of the eight wonders of the world. ( )

2. The "Hanging Gardens" is not a garden that floats in mid-air. ( )

11 How Were Roman Numerals Invented?

Roman numerals originated in Ancient Rome and were invented more than 2,000 years before Arabic numerals.

Initially, the Romans used their fingers as a tool for counting. To record different numbers, they drew "**I**," "**II**," and "**III**" on sheepskin, representing 1, 2, and 3 fingers they extended, respectively. To represent the fingers of one hand, they drew a "**V**" shape, like the position of the thumb and forefinger when opened; to represent the fingers of both hands, they drew a "**V V**" shape, which later became an "**X**" shape with one hand up and one hand down. These symbols were the embryonic form of Roman numerals.

Later, to represent larger numbers, the Romans invented several more symbols. They used "**C**" to

(1) Which of the following statements about Roman numerals is incorrect? ( )

A. Roman numerals originated from counting with fingers.

B. "M" represents 1,000 and comes from the Latin word "mille."

C. Roman numerals have ten basic symbols.

D. The symbol representing 10 in Roman numerals has changed over time.

represent 100 because "**C**" is the first letter of the Latin word "centum," which means 100 (the English word "century" comes from this); the symbol "**M**" represents 1,000 because "**M**" is the first letter of the Latin word "mille," which means 1,000. The symbol "**L**" (half of the letter "**C**") represents 50, and the letter "**D**" represents 500. Thus, Roman numerals have the following seven basic symbols:

I = 1　　V = 5

X = 10　　L = 50　　C = 100

D = 500　　M = 1,000

(2) Roman numerals have 7 basic symbols: ________.

(3) Judge true or false based on the article.

1. The Roman numeral "X" originated from the position of two hands on the left and right, representing 10. (　)

2. The letters "C" and "M" in Roman numerals come from Latin. (　)

12 World Architectural Wonder—the Colosseum

The Colosseum is located in Rome, the capital of Italy, symbolizing Ancient Roman civilization. Its original name was the Flavian Amphitheater, the Roman Colosseum, or the Arena.

The Colosseum is considered a great miracle in the history of world architecture. Its bottom level has 80 arches, forming 80 openings. Spectators have to take their seats according to their seat numbers. First, the audience needs to find the entrance through which they should enter from one of the bottom level arches; then, they need to find the area where their seat is located by following the stairs and passageways; and finally, they find their seat. The entire Colosseum can accommodate up to 90,000 people, but due to its well-designed layout, there will be no overcrowding or confusion. Later, many large sports

Challenge

(1) Why is the Colosseum considered the world's earliest large sports arena?

A. The first sports games were held here.

B. The entrance and exit design here meets the needs of large sports arenas.

C. The sports field design here meets the needs of large sports arenas.

D. The design of the arches outside the Colosseum meets the needs of large sports arenas.

stadiums borrowed from this design principle. It can be said that the Colosseum is the world's earliest large sports arena.

The Colosseum is surrounded by 240 arches on the outside. Arches are the most representative element of Roman architecture. The arch shape increases the span, and the weight is evenly distributed over the entire arch span, providing strong support for the building structure. It is both sturdy and magnificent, perfectly combining art and architecture. Nowadays, the English word "architect" is also closely related to the word "arch" for arches and is derived from the Latin word arcus.

Although the once majestic Colosseum now only has ruins and broken walls, it is still a gem in the treasure trove of world architectural art.

(2) The Colosseum is in Italy; its original name is _____.

(3) Judge true or false based on the article.

1. The Colosseum, the Arena, and the Flavian Amphitheater are in the same place. ( )

2. The English word "architect" derives from Roman words. ( )

13 Can Counting Rods Be Used to Calculate Negative Numbers?

In daily life, we often use negative numbers. For example, what is the new temperature if cold air comes and the temperature in a certain place was originally 4°C but drops by 10°C? If we use a formula to represent this, we need to find the difference between "4−10," and the answer is −6 °C (negative 6°C), which involves negative numbers.

Many people think that ancient people did not understand negative numbers, let alone how to calculate them. As early as the 3rd century BC, the ancient Chinese mathematician Liu Hui had already proposed the concept of negative numbers and creatively used red counting rods to represent positive numbers and black counting rods to represent negative numbers. The people of that era in China could already use counting rods to perform calculations involving negative numbers.

(1) Based on the article's content, guess what number the black counting rods represent.

A. 31 B. 13 C. −31 D. −13

(2) The part of an economic activity where expenses exceed income is called ________.

Today, this method of using colors to distinguish positive and negative still exists in daily life. For example, "red ink" (a deficit) refers to the difference in economic activity between expenditures and income and is usually written in red in account books to indicate a loss.

(3) Judge true or false based on the article.

1. The color used to represent negative numbers on counting rods is the same as that used to indicate a deficit in modern economic activity. ( )

2. During the Tang Dynasty (AD 618–907), the Chinese could use counting rods to calculate negative numbers. ( )

14 Colorful Terracotta Army

Today, if we visit Emperor Qinshihuang's Mausoleum Site Museum, the Terracotta Army we see is monotonously gray. However, the Terracotta Army made by the people of the Qin Dynasty (221–207 BC) was not this color but was covered in various intense colors like red, green, purple, yellow, and so on.

Why did the excavated terracotta warriors turn gray? Some experts have said, "The humidity and temperature underground protected the color of the cultural relics. Once the relics are excavated, the surface will quickly lose water, the paint will curl and peel off rapidly, and the color will disappear." Environmental change is the main reason for the rapid fading of the Terracotta Army.

At the beginning of the discovery of the Terracotta Army, the scientific technology at that time was not capable of maintaining the splendid color of the Terracotta Army.

Challenge

(1) Which of the following statements about the Terracotta Army is correct? (   )

A. The Terracotta Army in the museum looks the same as when it was first made.

B. The buried Terracotta Army is not gray.

C. We can now see the excavated colorful Terracotta Army in the museum.

D. Scientists still need help to maintain the color of the Terracotta Army.

To make up for the regret of the Terracotta Army's rapid fading, scientists from China and abroad have carried out years of research and have basically solved the problem of maintaining the surface color of the Terracotta Army. However, these colorful Qin terracotta warriors have yet to be exhibited and are unavailable for visitors.

(2) ________ is the main reason for the Terracotta Army's rapid fading.

(3) Judge true or false based on the article.

1. *The people of the Qin Dynasty were able to make various colors of pigments.* ( )

2. *The excavated Terracotta Army has all turned gray.* ( )

15 Why Does the Sun Rise in the East and Set in the West?

In the morning, the sun rises from the east; in the evening, it sets to the west. This is not because the sun revolves around earth but because earth rotates on its axis.

Earth's rotation refers to earth's constant west-to-east motion around its axis. Although we live on earth, it is very large, and it isn't easy to perceive its rotation. This is similar to the experience of flying in an airplane. We hardly feel it moving forward when the plane is flying (except during takeoff, landing, and turbulence).

Imagine this scenario: You are sitting on a carousel, and your mom is waving at you from the outer edge. As the carousel spins, your mom's figure moves backward until you can no longer see her, but soon enough, you can see your mom again.

Earth is like a carousel, constantly rotating, while the stationary mom represents the sun. The direction

(1) Based on the article's content, we would see the sun if earth rotates from east to west ( ).

A. Rise from the west and set to the east

B. Rise from the east and set to the west

C. Rise from the east and set to the east

D. Rise from the west and set to the west

of earth's rotation is from west to east, with one full rotation in a day. Therefore, from earth's perspective, the sun appears to rise from the east, move across the sky from east to west, and then set to the west.

(2) We see the sunrise in the east and set in the west because ________.

(3) Judge true or false based on the article.

1. *The direction of earth's rotation is from west to east. ( )*
2. *When you cannot see the sun, people in other parts of earth cannot see the sun either. ( )*

16 The Origin of the Name of Sanxingdui

The Sanxingdui site, which has a history of 3,000 to 5,000 years, is the most culturally rich Ancient Shu civilization site discovered in southwest China. Tens of thousands of precious bronze artifacts, such as bronze human figurines, bronze divine trees, and bronze masks, have been unearthed there.

Where does the name Sanxingdui come from? A long time ago, 3 large loess mounds were near the current Sanxingdui site. Across from these mounds, separated by the Mamu River, is a very high terrace shaped like a crescent moon called the Moon Bay Terrace. The Moon Bay Terrace and the 3 loess mounds facing each other across the river form a famous natural landscape in the area called "*Sanxing Ban Yue Dui*" (3 star-shaped mounds next to the crescent moon), which is the origin of the name Sanxingdui.

(1) The name of the Sanxingdui site comes from ( ).

A. People's worship of stars in the sky

B. The nearby attraction "Sanxing Ban Yue Dui"

C. Three bronze objects in the shape of stars excavated from here

D. The name of the first discoverer

According to the naming principles of archaeology, typical sites that are first discovered are usually named after the local place names, such as the Zhoukoudian site, Yangshao Culture site, Dawenkou Culture site, and Hemudu Culture site. The Sanxingdui site was discovered near the "*Sanxing Ban Yue Dui*." According to the principle of naming after local place names, it was named "Sanxingdui."

(2) The Sanxingdui site is a culturally rich _____ site in southwest China.

(3) Judge true or false based on the article.

1. Archaeologists usually name sites after the province where they were discovered. ( )

2. The bronze divine tree is an artifact unearthed from the Sanxingdui site. ( )

17 Why Does the Moon Phase Keep Changing?

If you often observe the moon, you will find that the shape of the bright part of the moon, known as the moon phase, keeps changing at different times of the month. Sometimes the moon looks like a sickle, and sometimes it looks like a big jade plate. Why does it happen?

In fact, the moon itself does not emit light. We can see the moonlight because the moon reflects sunlight. Also, the moon revolves around earth, so the sunlight will shine on the moon from different angles. When we look at the moon from earth, we naturally see the changing moon phase.

After night falls, we can do a little experiment. First, turn on a desk lamp and use it as the sun. Then, lift a ball and use it as the moon, while you represent earth. When the ball is exactly between the desk lamp and

Challenge

(1) When might we see a full moon? (   ) (Select all that apply)

A. When the moon is between earth and the sun

B. When the moon is farthest from the sun

C. When the moon is closest to the sun

D. When earth is between the moon and the sun but smaller

(2) When the moon is between earth and the sun, the moon phase is _____.

you, the surface facing you becomes the dark side, and it cannot be illuminated by the desk lamp. This is the principle of the new moon. As we slowly rotate, the light will gradually shine on the side of the ball, and as it rotates, the illuminated part of the ball will become more and more. Until we turn our back to the desk lamp, and the light will shine on the entire surface of the ball. This is the principle of the full moon.

The moon revolves around earth for about a month. Therefore, the moon phase we see on earth is constantly changing during a month, and its changing pattern is from the new moon to the full moon and back to new moon.

(3) Judge true or false based on the article.

1. The moonlight we see comes from the sunlight emitted by the sun. ( )

2. It takes a month from the new moon to the full moon. ( )

18 Why Can't We See the Dark Side of the Moon?

Usually, we call the side of the moon facing earth the front side and the other side the dark side. On earth, we can never see the dark side of the moon. This is because the moon's rotation period is basically the same as its revolution period. In astronomy, this phenomenon is called tidal locking.

We can imagine the spinning motion of a hammer thrower when they throw the hammer. The athlete's chain locks the hammer like earth's gravity tidally locks the moon. The side of the hammer facing the athlete is always the side with the chain attached, and the athlete can only see that side of the hammer. Similarly, on earth, we can only see the front side of the moon forever.

So, do we have no chance to see the "back of the head" of the moon? Currently, humans have launched

Challenge

(1) The dark side of the moon is ( ).

A. The side facing away from the sun
B. The side not illuminated by sunlight
C. Yet to be explored by any probe
D. The side facing away from earth

(2) The phenomenon where the rotation period of a celestial body is roughly the same as its revolution period is called ______ in astronomy.

moon rovers to explore the dark side of the moon. China's Chang'e 4 lunar rover was the first soft-landing probe to land on the moon's dark side launched by humans. It transmitted the world's first close-up image of the moon's backside, allowing people to see the "back of the head" of the moon.

(3) Judge true or false based on the article.

1. *Humans still have no information about the dark side of the moon.* ( )

2. *Due to tidal locking, the moon no longer rotates.* ( )

19 Astronomical Seasons and Meteorological Seasons

The traditional way of dividing the four seasons in China is to use the "4 beginnings" of the 24 solar terms as the starting point of the seasons and use the "2 solstices" and "2 equinoxes" as the midpoints of the seasons. For example, the Beginning of Spring is the starting point of spring, and the Summer Solstice is the midpoint of summer. These are the astronomical seasons based on the height of the sun and the length of day and night.

However, the amount of sunlight received by different parts of the earth is different, and the amount of solar heat received is also different. Therefore, the seasonal changes and temperatures in different regions also vary greatly. For example, in October every year, children in Heilongjiang Province (Northeast China) have already put on thick coats, while children in Hainan Province (Southern China) can still wear short sleeves. Therefore, meteorologists

(1) Which of the following statements regarding astronomical and meteorological seasons is correct? ( )

A. They are the same division method.

B. Astronomical seasons are divided based on the average temperature.

C. Meteorological seasons are divided based on the height of the sun.

D. The 24 solar terms are closely related to astronomical seasons.

have developed the "meteorological seasons." The meteorological seasons are divided based on the average temperature. This method defines the period with an average temperature greater than or equal to 22°C as summer, the period with an average temperature less than or equal to 10°C as winter, and the period between 10°C and 22°C as spring or autumn.

Therefore, the division of astronomical seasons depends on the changes in astronomical phenomena, while the division of meteorological seasons depends on the changes in temperature.

(2) The period recognized as summer by meteorology is when the average temperature is greater than or equal to ______ °C.

(3) Judge true or false based on the article.

1. When the Beginning of Summer arrives, all parts of the country enter the meteorological summer. ( )

2. The Summer Solstice is the midpoint of summer in astronomical seasons. ( )

20 Where Does the Sun Never Set?

The sun only rises and sets once a year at the South Pole and the North Pole on earth. There is half a year when the sun never sets; it is always daytime and is called polar day. There is also half a year when the sun cannot be seen; it is always nighttime and is called polar night.

Polar day and polar night are unique natural phenomena within the polar circles. This natural phenomenon is because the earth rotates around the sun with a tilted axis. During the earth's rotation around the sun, the South Pole faces the sun for 6 months, while the North Pole always faces away from the sun. The situation is reversed for the other 6 months. On June 22 of each year, when the sun's rays move to the Tropic of Cancer, the entire Arctic Circle can be illuminated by the sun for 24 hours. On December 22 of each year, when the sun's rays move to

Challenge

(1) The main reason for the polar day and night phenomenon is ( ).

A. The South and North Poles are too cold, and the reflection of ice and snow gives people a wrong impression.

B. Sunlight refracts in the universe.

C. Earth revolves around the sun while also rotating around its tilted axis.

D. The distance between the earth and the sun changes during the earth's rotation around the sun.

the Tropic of Capricorn, the entire Antarctic Circle can be illuminated by the sun for 24 hours.

Svalbard, Norway's Sommarøy Island is located in a special geographic location north of the Arctic Circle. From May 18 to July 26 every year, the island experiences 69 days of polar day and can be said to be the true "city on which the sun never sets."

(2) Within a day, the sun is always above the horizon, and it is daylight for 24 hours. This phenomenon is called ( ).

A. Polar day | *B. Polar night*

C. Pole | *D. South and North Pole*

(3) Judge true or false based on the article.

1. Only Sommarøy Island has the phenomenon of polar day and night. ( )

2. On December 22, the North Pole is in the polar day period. ( )

21 Why Is a Quarter of 1 Hour Called 15 Minutes?

There may be different ways to express the same moment in daily life. For example, when some say "2:15," others say, "quarter past two," which means the same thing. So why is 15 minutes also "a quarter of an hour?"

China is one of the earliest countries to invent timekeeping devices. In different historical periods, the Chinese invented various timekeeping tools, such as the *gui* (a tool for determining the seasons, dividing the seasons, and calculating the calendar based on changes in the length of the sun's shadow), the sundial, a horological (measuring time) device that tells the time of day when direct sunlight shines by the apparent position of the sun in the sky, and the *louke* (a water clock, a type of ancient timekeeper).

The principle of the *louke* is simple. Water flows out of a small hole at the bottom of the pot when it is filled with

(1) Chinese people call 15 minutes "a quarter of an hour" because ( ).

A. Sundials are carved with a knife

B. Each scale of arrow mark on the louke represents 15 minutes

C. The inventor of the louke made this rule

D. Current national laws make a clear requirement

water. If all the water in the pot can be drained in one day and one night, 24 hours have passed. The 100 marks on the *louke* are evenly divided into 24 hours, with each mark representing 14.4 minutes.

Later, the Qing Dynasty (AD 1636–1912) issued a law on time scales, which changed the 100 marks on the *louke* to 96 marks. As a result, "a quarter of an hour" represented exactly 15 minutes. This way of expressing time has been passed down to this day.

Bronze *louke* from the Western Han Dynasty (206 BC–AD 25)

(2) 4:45 can be expressed as ( ). (Select all that apply)

A. A quarter to 5   B. 3-quarters past 4
C. 2-quarters past 4   D. A quarter to 4

(3) Judge true or false based on the article.

1. The scale of arrow mark on the *louke* has never changed since its invention. ( )

2. The *gui*, sundial, and *louke* are all ancient timekeeping tools in China. ( )

22 What Time Is "*San Geng Banye*"?

Chinese people often use the phrase "*san geng banye*" (三更半夜) to indicate it's late at night. So, what time exactly does "*san geng banye*" refer to?

In ancient China, people created a separate unit of time for the long night, called a "*geng*" (更). One night was divided into five "*geng*," each "*geng*" being 2 hours long.

The times for each "*geng*" are as follows: the 1st "*geng*" is from 7 p.m. to 9 p.m.; the 2nd "*geng*" is from 10 p.m. to 11 p.m.; the 3rd "*geng*" is from 11 p.m. to 1 a.m.; the 4th "*geng*" is from 1 a.m. to 3 a.m.; and the 5th "*geng*" is from 3 a.m. to 5 a.m. Therefore, "*san geng*" (三更) refers to the time between 11 p.m. and 1 a.m., and "*banye*" (半夜 [midnight]) refers to the middle "*geng*" among the 5 "*geng*," which is "*san*

Challenge

(I) In the idioms below, ( ) is a phrase composed of two synonyms, just like "*san geng banye.*"

A. Jian duo shi guang (见多识广) (This phrase means "seen much, know much." It is used to describe someone who has a wide range of knowledge and experiences.)

B. Cai gao ba dou (才高八斗) (This phrase means that one's talent is as much as eight bushels. It describes someone very talented or skilled in a particular area.)

C. Man fu jing lun (满腹经纶) (This phrase means "full belly of classic works." It is used to describe someone who has a wealth

geng." Thus, "*san geng*" and "*banye*" have the same meaning.

Therefore, the phrase "*san geng banye*" is composed of two synonyms, "*san geng*" and "*banye*." In ancient Chinese poetry, "*san geng*" frequently appeared as a time word.

of knowledge and is well-read in various classic works.)

D. Chu kou cheng zhang (出口成章) (This phrase means "spoken words become a chapter." It describes someone eloquent and articulate, able to express themselves effectively and beautifully.)

(2) Ancient Chinese people created a separate unit of time for the night called "________."

(3) Judge true or false based on the article.

1. *"San geng" and "banye" refer to different times.* ( )
2. *Midnight can be called "san geng banye."* ( )

23 Why Do Clock Hands Rotate in a Clockwise Direction?

Why do clock hands always rotate clockwise, whether they turn forward or backward? Doesn't one rotation of the hour hand represent the passing of 12 hours?

We have to start with the predecessor of clocks. Before the advent of clocks, people used a timekeeping tool called *ri gui* (日晷 [sundial]). "*Ri*" (日) means sun, and "*gui*" (晷) means sun's shadow. *Ri gui* is an instrument that uses the sun's shadow to indicate time. The sundial looks somewhat similar to the clocks we use today. It has a dial called a sundial surface, marked with scales and a sundial needle. However, the needle does not move; its shadow moves with time and indicates the time.

In the Northern Hemisphere, the shadow of the needle on a sundial changes direction this way: in the early morning, the needle's shadow points west when the sun rises in the east. As the sun gradually rises, the shadow

Challenge

(1) According to the article, which of the following statements is incorrect? (   )

A. When the sun is in the east, the shadow of a sundial needle points to the west.

B. Modern mechanical clocks first appeared in Europe.

C. In the Southern Hemisphere, the sun rises in the west and sets in the east.

D. The direction of the shadow's movement on a sundial is opposite in the Northern and Southern Hemispheres.

slowly moves north. In the afternoon, the shadow gradually points eastward again. Therefore, the needle's shadow on a sundial must move clockwise in the Northern Hemisphere. Of course, if the sundial were in the Southern Hemisphere, the direction of the shadow's movement would be completely different.

Mechanical clocks first appeared in Europe, in the Northern Hemisphere. Modern clock hands rotate clockwise because Europeans designed clocks to mimic the movement of the sundial's shadow.

(2) The direction of the movement of the clock hands is modeled after the movement of the shadow of _____.

(3) Judge true or false based on the article.

1. In the Southern Hemisphere, the shadow of a sundial moves counterclockwise. ( )

2. People from the Southern Hemisphere invented modern clocks. ( )

24 Which Countries Have the 12 Zodiac Signs?

The zodiac, the Chinese horoscope, is often used to record a person's birth year. The Chinese Zodiac represents the 12 earthly branches: Rat, Ox, Tiger, Rabbit, Dragon, Snake, Horse, Goat, Monkey, Rooster, Dog, and Pig.

In fact, besides China, many other countries also have a zodiac culture. Among them, the zodiac cultures of many Asian countries are deeply influenced by Chinese culture.

North Korea, South Korea, and Japan are close to China, and Singapore has a large Chinese population, so the zodiac cultures of these countries are the same as China's. The 12 zodiac signs in Thailand and Cambodia are the same as in China, but the order differs. Thailand's zodiac order starts with the Snake and ends with the Dragon, while Cambodia's zodiac

Challenge

(1) According to the article, which statement is incorrect? (   )

A. Children in Kazakhstan may belong to the snail zodiac.

B. Children in Vietnam may belong to the rabbit zodiac.

C. Children in Egypt may belong to the crab zodiac.

D. Children in Mexico may belong to the lizard zodiac.

sign order starts with the Ox and ends with the Rat. Vietnam's 12 zodiac animals only differ from China's by replacing "Rabbit" with "Cat."

Some countries have included animals with local characteristics in their 12 zodiac signs. For example, zodiac signs in Mexico includes lizards, Egypt includes crabs, and Kazakhstan includes snails. It can be seen that the popular and interesting zodiac cultures have become an indispensable part of folk culture in many countries.

(2) 2024 is the Year of the Dragon in China. So, the next Year of the Dragon in China is ______.

(3) Judge true or false based on the article.

1. *The 12 zodiac signs in different countries are not the same. ( )*

2. *Thailand's zodiac sign is the same as China's. ( )*

25 How Many Constellations Are in the Sky?

We can discover constellations if we divide the starry sky into several regions, connect the stars in each region with lines, and associate them with familiar objects. Some constellations look like animals, such as Aries; some look like objects, such as Lyra; and some look like mythical figures, such as Ophiuchus. So, how many constellations are there in the sky?

Around 1000 BC, the Ancient Babylonians proposed 30 constellations by observing the starry sky. The names of some constellations we often mention nowadays, such as Aquarius, Taurus, and Libra, are all derived from the names of the Ancient Babylonians.

In the 2nd century AD, the Greek astronomer Ptolemy synthesized the astronomical achievements of his time, compiled 48 constellations, and connected the brightest stars in each constellation with imaginary lines. He then

Challenge

(1) According to the information published by the International Astronomical Union, how many constellations are in the sky?

A. 30 B. 48 C. 88 D. 12

(2) The Ancient Greek astronomer ______ compiled 48 constellations and recorded them.

imagined them as animal or human shapes and gave them appropriate names combined with mythical stories. Ptolemy recorded 1,022 stars in these 48 constellations in his book *Almagest*, the prototype of modern constellations. Later astronomers added new constellations based on Ptolemy's constellations.

In 1928, the International Astronomical Union officially announced that there are 88 constellations in the sky, 28 of which are in the Northern Hemisphere, 48 in the Southern Hemisphere, and 12 near the celestial equator and ecliptic.

(3) Judge true or false based on the article.

1. *Constellations are all named after human or animal names. ( )*
2. *Ptolemy named all the constellations in the sky today. ( )*

26 The Brightest Star in the Night Sky

When we look at the night sky, we must wonder which star is the brightest.

To measure the brightness of celestial bodies in the night sky, the Ancient Greek astronomer Hipparchus proposed the concept of "magnitude." He divided stars into 6 magnitudes, with the brightest star being the first and the dimmest being the sixth. What he called "magnitude" was actually visual magnitude, referring to the brightness of stars observed with the naked eye on earth.

In 1850, British astronomer Norman Pogson discovered that the brightness of a first-magnitude star is about 100 times that of a sixth-magnitude star. He further quantified it: stars brighter than the first magnitude can have magnitudes less than one, even negative magnitudes.

So, which is the brightest star in the night sky? Late at night, the brightest star in the night sky should be Sirius,

Challenge

(1) Which of the following statements is correct regarding visual magnitude in astronomy?

A. Visual magnitude refers to the true brightness of celestial bodies.

B. Visual magnitude refers to the brightness of celestial bodies observed by people on the earth.

C. Visual magnitude is divided only into 6 levels from 1 to 6.

D. Visual magnitude has nothing to do with the distance between celestial bodies and the earth.

with a magnitude of −1.45. However, the visual magnitude cannot represent the true brightness of celestial bodies, as the brightness of stars depends largely on their distance from the earth. Sirius is large and relatively close to the earth, so it appears brighter.

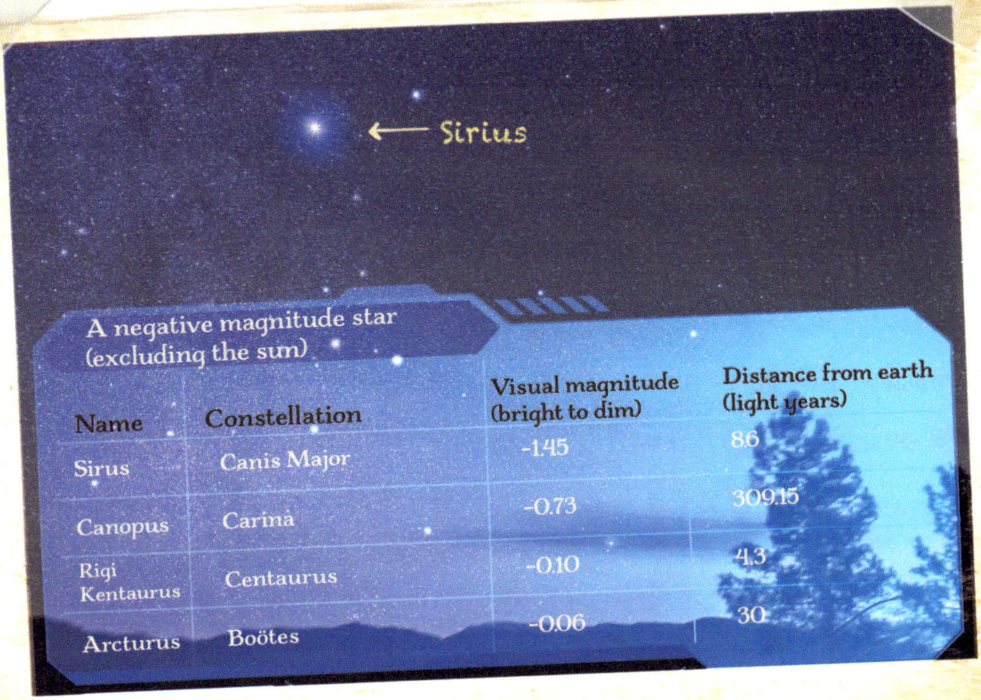

A negative magnitude star (excluding the sun)

Name	Constellation	Visual magnitude (bright to dim)	Distance from earth (light years)
Sirus	Canis Major	-1.45	8.6
Canopus	Carina	-0.73	309.15
Riqi Kentaurus	Centaurus	-0.10	4.3
Arcturus	Boötes	-0.06	30

(2) In late night, the brightest star on the earth is ________.

(3) Judge true or false based on the article.

1. *Visual magnitude can be negative.* ( )

2. *The brightness of stars depends only on their distance from the earth.* ( )

27 Where Will a Compass Point to at the South Pole?

We all know that a compass can indicate the north and south directions. So, how would the compass indicate direction if we were at the southernmost point of the earth, the South Pole?

Earth is like a huge magnet, with south and north magnetic poles. However, the geographic South Pole and earth's south magnetic poles do not coincide. The south magnetic pole is about 1,600 km northeast of the South Pole, and its position moves 10–15 km yearly. There is an angle of about 11°C between earth's magnetic and rotational axes (earth's axis). Therefore, the compass does not point to the true south or north direction, but to the direction of the magnetic poles.

So, if we place a compass at the South Pole, its pointer will naturally point to the south magnetic pole

Challenge

(1) The south magnetic pole refers to the southern end of earth's magnetic field, and it is currently ( ). (Select all that apply)

A. Located near the South Pole of earth

B. Located near the North Pole of earth

C. Located near the equator of earth

D. Constantly moving

in its northeast direction. If we place the compass at the south magnetic pole, it will lose its horizontal tension and have no fixed direction so that it will rotate freely.

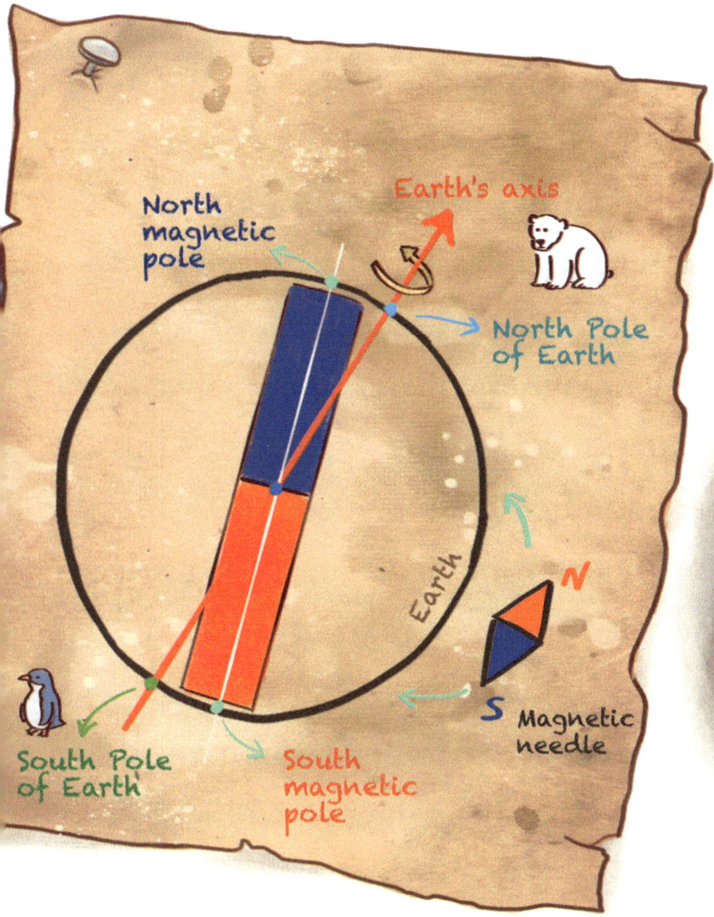

(2) There is an angle of _____ between earth's magnetic and rotational axes.

(3) Judge true or false based on the article.

1. The position of the south magnetic pole is fixed and located 1,600 km northeast of the South Pole. ( )

2. The north magnetic pole coincides with the geographic North Pole. ( )

28 Can Magnets Fail?

If we burn a magnet in a flame for more than 5 minutes, it will fail and can no longer pick up small iron nails. Isn't this phenomenon amazing?

At the end of the 19th century, the famous physicist Pierre Curie (husband of Madam Curie) discovered a physical property of a magnet in his laboratory, which is that the magnetism of a magnet will disappear when heated to a certain temperature. Later, people called this temperature the Curie point or Curie temperature.

The reason why magnets have magnetism is that the atoms inside the magnet are arranged in a very regular manner. However, when the magnet is heated and reaches a certain temperature, the atoms arranged regularly inside the magnet will be disturbed, and the magnet will lose its original magnetism.

Challenge

(1) Which of the following statements is incorrect according to the article's content?

A. The Curie point of each magnetic material is different.

B. The main reason for the failure of magnets is that the arrangement of atoms inside the magnet is disrupted.

C. Madam Curie was the first to discover the phenomenon of magnets failing when heated.

D. The Curie point has been applied to daily appliances.

Electric rice cookers can automatically keep warm, which utilizes the property of magnets losing magnetism when heated. The center of the bottom of the electric rice cooker is equipped with a magnet and a magnetic material with a Curie point of 105°C. When the rice is cooked, the temperature in the pot rises. When the temperature reaches 105°C, the spring between the magnet and the magnetic material will separate them, thereby automatically cutting off the power to prevent the rice from burning.

Magnets have magnetism (Internal magnetic field direction is consistent with the external magnetic field direction.)

Magnets lose their magnetism (The internal magnetic field is disordered.)

(2) The physical property that the magnetism of a magnet disappears when it is heated to a certain temperature was discovered by ______.

(3) Judge true or false based on the article.

1. *The atoms inside the magnet are arranged in an orderly manner.* ( )
2. *Madam Curie's husband was also a physicist.* ( )